MW00593637

THE
GARDENER'S
LOGBOOK

PETER PAUPER PRESS, INC.
WHITE PLAINS, NEW YORK

PETER PAUPER PRESS
Fine Books and Gifts Since 1928

OUR COMPANY

In 1928, at the age of twenty-two, Peter Beilenson began printing books on a small press in the basement of his parents' home in Larchmont, New York. Peter—and later, his wife, Edna—sought to create fine books that sold at "prices even a pauper could afford."

Today, still family owned and operated, Peter Pauper Press continues to honor our founders' legacy—and our customers' expectations—of beauty, quality, and value.

Cover image used under license from Shutterstock.com
Designed by Margaret Rubiano

Copyright © 2020
Peter Pauper Press, Inc.
202 Mamaroneck Avenue
White Plains, NY 10601 USA
All rights reserved
ISBN 978-1-4413-3278-3
Printed in China
7 6 5 4 3 2

Visit us at www.peterpauper.com

CONTENTS

INTRODUCTION

> *What it takes humans a lifetime to experience,*
> *a plant will experience in its own yearly life cycle.*
> *In that sense, gardening is a microcosm of life.*
>
> PIET OUDOLF

Whether you're planning a patio container garden, a succulent garden, a backyard veggie patch, or a lush meadow garden adrift with ornamental grasses, this logbook can help. Track each plant you choose, from its beginnings in your garden, through the growing season, and beyond. Note successes for next year. Note what didn't work and why, so you won't repeat mistakes. Tuck photos, seed packets, plant labels, and garden center receipts within the inside back cover pocket. We've included some general tips and suggestions as well, plus helpful websites and dot matrix grid pages for laying out your vision. Get the most from your garden!

PLANT LOG

PLANT NAME Pumpkins

SCIENTIFIC NAME

Flower ☐ Vegetable ☒ Fruit ☐ Herb ☐ Shrub ☐ Tree ☐

(Annual) ☐ Biennial ☐ Perennial ☐ Seedling ☐ Bulb ☐

SUPPLIER Burpee   **COST**

Date Germinated Seeds   Date Planted 5 -29

Location _____ Sun ☑ Partial Sun ☐ Shade ☐

Fertilizer/Soil Amendment Plant food

Pests/Weeds/Control Castor oil/Dishsoap

Watering/Rainfall Water almost everyday

Date Bloomed/Harvested

Notes

Rate It: (1) (2) (3) (4) (5)

~~~~~ PLANT LOG ~~~~~

PLANT NAME Sweet Potato

SCIENTIFIC NAME

Flower ☐ (Vegetable ☐) Fruit ☐ Herb ☐ Shrub ☐ Tree ☐
Annual ☐ Biennial ☐ Perennial ☐ Seedling ☐ Bulb ☐

SUPPLIER Burpee   COST

Date Germinated Bare Roots   Date Planted 5-29

Location _____ Sun ☑ Partial Sun ☐ Shade ☐

Fertilizer/Soil Amendment Plant food

Pests/Weeds/Control Castor oil/Dish Soap

Watering/Rainfall Almost Everyday

Date Bloomed/Harvested

Notes

Rate It: (1)   (2)   (3)   (4)   (5)

🌿 PLANT LOG 🌿

PLANT NAME Cucumbers

SCIENTIFIC NAME

Flower ☐ Vegetable ☐ (Fruit ✓) Herb ☐ Shrub ☐ Tree ☐

Annual ☐ Biennial ☐ Perennial ☐ Seedling ☐ Bulb ☐

SUPPLIER .... **COST** ....

Date Germinated Seeds Date Planted 5-29-21

Location .... Sun ✓ Partial Sun ☐ Shade ☐

Fertilizer/Soil Amendment Plant Food

Pests/Weeds/Control Castor oil/Dish soap

Watering/Rainfall Almost everyday

Date Bloomed/Harvested

Notes

Rate It: (1) (2) (3) (4) (5)

🌾 PLANT LOG 🌾

PLANT NAME Carrots

SCIENTIFIC NAME

Flower ☐ Vegetable (✓) Fruit ☐ Herb ☐ Shrub ☐ Tree ☐

Annual ☐ Biennial ☐ Perennial ☐ Seedling ☐ Bulb ☐

SUPPLIER Burpee   **COST**

Date Germinated Seeds   Date Planted 5-29-21

Location _____ Sun ☑ Partial Sun ☐ Shade ☐

Fertilizer/Soil Amendment Plant food

Pests/Weeds/Control Castor oil / Dish Soap

Watering/Rainfall Almost Everyday

Date Bloomed/Harvested

Notes

Rate It: (1) (2) (3) (4) (5)

✿✿✿ PLANT LOG ✿✿✿

PLANT NAME Peas

SCIENTIFIC NAME

Flower ☐ Vegetable ☑ Fruit ☐ Herb ☐ Shrub ☐ Tree ☐
Annual ☐ Biennial ☐ Perennial ☐ Seedling ☐ Bulb ☐

SUPPLIER Burpee   **COST**

Date Germinated Seeds   Date Planted 5-29-21

Location .... Sun ☑ Partial Sun ☐ Shade ☐

Fertilizer/Soil Amendment

Pests/Weeds/Control

Watering/Rainfall

Date Bloomed/Harvested

Notes

Rate It: (1)   (2)   (3)   (4)   (5)

✿✿✿✿ PLANT LOG ✿✿✿✿

PLANT NAME _Beans_

SCIENTIFIC NAME

Flower ☐ Vegetable ☐ Fruit ☐ Herb ☐ Shrub ☐ Tree ☐

Annual ☐ Biennial ☐ Perennial ☐ Seedling ☐ Bulb ☐

SUPPLIER _Burpee_   COST

Date Germinated _Seeds_   Date Planted _5-29-21_

Location .... Sun ☑ Partial Sun ☐ Shade ☐

Fertilizer/Soil Amendment

Pests/Weeds/Control

Watering/Rainfall

Date Bloomed/Harvested

Notes

Rate It: (1)   (2)   (3)   (4)   (5)

✿✿✿✿ PLANT LOG ✿✿✿✿

PLANT NAME *Peppers*

SCIENTIFIC NAME

Flower ☐ Vegetable ☐ Fruit ☐ Herb ☐ Shrub ☐ Tree ☐

Annual ☐ Biennial ☐ Perennial ☐ Seedling ☐ Bulb ☐

SUPPLIER _____ **COST** _____

Date Germinated *Plants* Date Planted *5-29-21*

Location _____ Sun ☑ Partial Sun ☐ Shade ☐

Fertilizer/Soil Amendment _____

Pests/Weeds/Control _____

_____

Watering/Rainfall _____

_____

Date Bloomed/Harvested _____

Notes _____

_____

_____

Rate It: 1 2 3 4 5

PLANT LOG

PLANT NAME Tomatoes

SCIENTIFIC NAME

Flower ☐ Vegetable ☐ Fruit ☑ Herb ☐ Shrub ☐ Tree ☐

Annual ☐ Biennial ☐ Perennial ☐ Seedling ☐ Bulb ☐

SUPPLIER Burpee/mike Bonnie **COST**

Date Germinated plants Date Planted 5-29-21

Location ____ Sun ☐ Partial Sun ☐ Shade ☐

Fertilizer/Soil Amendment

Pests/Weeds/Control

Watering/Rainfall

Date Bloomed/Harvested

Notes

Rate It: ① ② ③ ④ ⑤

12

🌿 PLANT LOG 🌿

PLANT NAME **Sunflowers**

SCIENTIFIC NAME

Flower ☐ Vegetable ☐ Fruit ☐ Herb ☐ Shrub ☐ Tree ☐

Annual ☐ Biennial ☐ Perennial ☐ Seedling ☐ Bulb ☐

SUPPLIER **Burpee**   COST

Date Germinated **Seeds**   Date Planted **5-29-21**

Location .... Sun ☑ Partial Sun ☐ Shade ☐

Fertilizer/Soil Amendment

Pests/Weeds/Control

Watering/Rainfall

Date Bloomed/Harvested

Notes

Rate It: (1)   (2)   (3)   (4)   (5)

❧ PLANT LOG ❧

PLANT NAME ....

SCIENTIFIC NAME ....
Flower ☐ Vegetable ☐ Fruit ☐ Herb ☐ Shrub ☐ Tree ☐
Annual ☐ Biennial ☐ Perennial ☐ Seedling ☐ Bulb ☐

SUPPLIER .... **COST** ....

Date Germinated .... Date Planted ....

Location .... Sun ☐ Partial Sun ☐ Shade ☐

Fertilizer/Soil Amendment ....

Pests/Weeds/Control ....

....

Watering/Rainfall..

....

Date Bloomed/Harvested ....

Notes ....

....

....

Rate It: (1) (2) (3) (4) (5)

❧❧ PLANT LOG ❧❧

PLANT NAME ....

SCIENTIFIC NAME ....

Flower ☐ Vegetable ☐ Fruit ☐ Herb ☐ Shrub ☐ Tree ☐

Annual ☐ Biennial ☐ Perennial ☐ Seedling ☐ Bulb ☐

SUPPLIER .... **COST** ....

Date Germinated .... Date Planted ....

Location .... Sun ☐ Partial Sun ☐ Shade ☐

Fertilizer/Soil Amendment ....

Pests/Weeds/Control ....

....

Watering/Rainfall ....

....

Date Bloomed/Harvested ....

Notes ....

....

....

Rate It: (1) (2) (3) (4) (5)

❀❀❀ PLANT LOG ❀❀❀

PLANT NAME ....

SCIENTIFIC NAME ....

Flower ☐ Vegetable ☐ Fruit ☐ Herb ☐ Shrub ☐ Tree ☐

Annual ☐ Biennial ☐ Perennial ☐ Seedling ☐ Bulb ☐

SUPPLIER .... **COST** ....

Date Germinated .... Date Planted ....

Location .... Sun ☐ Partial Sun ☐ Shade ☐

Fertilizer/Soil Amendment ....

Pests/Weeds/Control ....

....

Watering/Rainfall...

....

Date Bloomed/Harvested ....

Notes ....

....

....

Rate It: (1) (2) (3) (4) (5)

✿✿✿✿ PLANT LOG ✿✿✿✿

PLANT NAME ....

SCIENTIFIC NAME ....

   Flower ☐ Vegetable ☐ Fruit ☐ Herb ☐ Shrub ☐ Tree ☐

   Annual ☐ Biennial ☐ Perennial ☐ Seedling ☐ Bulb ☐

SUPPLIER .... **COST** ....

Date Germinated .... Date Planted ....

Location .... Sun ☐ Partial Sun ☐ Shade ☐

Fertilizer/Soil Amendment ....

Pests/Weeds/Control ....

....

Watering/Rainfall ....

....

Date Bloomed/Harvested ....

Notes ....

....

....

Rate It: (1) (2) (3) (4) (5)

❧ PLANT LOG ❧

PLANT NAME ....

SCIENTIFIC NAME ....

Flower ☐ Vegetable ☐ Fruit ☐ Herb ☐ Shrub ☐ Tree ☐

Annual ☐ Biennial ☐ Perennial ☐ Seedling ☐ Bulb ☐

SUPPLIER .... **COST** ....

Date Germinated .... Date Planted ....

Location .... Sun ☐ Partial Sun ☐ Shade ☐

Fertilizer/Soil Amendment ....

Pests/Weeds/Control ....

....

Watering/Rainfall ....

....

Date Bloomed/Harvested ....

Notes ....

....

....

Rate It: (1)   (2)   (3)   (4)   (5)

❧❧❧ PLANT LOG ❧❧❧

PLANT NAME ....

SCIENTIFIC NAME ....

    Flower ☐ Vegetable ☐ Fruit ☐ Herb ☐ Shrub ☐ Tree ☐

    Annual ☐ Biennial ☐ Perennial ☐ Seedling ☐ Bulb ☐

SUPPLIER ....   **COST** ....

Date Germinated...................................... Date Planted.................................

Location .... Sun ☐ Partial Sun ☐ Shade ☐

Fertilizer/Soil Amendment ....

Pests/Weeds/Control ....

....

Watering/Rainfall..

....

Date Bloomed/Harvested ....

Notes ....

....

....

Rate It: (1) (2) (3) (4) (5)

⚙ PLANT LOG ⚙

PLANT NAME ....

SCIENTIFIC NAME ....

Flower ☐ Vegetable ☐ Fruit ☐ Herb ☐ Shrub ☐ Tree ☐

Annual ☐ Biennial ☐ Perennial ☐ Seedling ☐ Bulb ☐

SUPPLIER .... **COST** ....

Date Germinated .... Date Planted ....

Location .... Sun ☐ Partial Sun ☐ Shade ☐

Fertilizer/Soil Amendment ....

Pests/Weeds/Control ....

....

Watering/Rainfall ....

....

Date Bloomed/Harvested ....

Notes ....

....

....

Rate It: (1) (2) (3) (4) (5)

PLANT LOG

PLANT NAME ....

SCIENTIFIC NAME ....

Flower ☐ Vegetable ☐ Fruit ☐ Herb ☐ Shrub ☐ Tree ☐

Annual ☐ Biennial ☐ Perennial ☐ Seedling ☐ Bulb ☐

SUPPLIER .... **COST** ....

Date Germinated .... Date Planted ....

Location .... Sun ☐ Partial Sun ☐ Shade ☐

Fertilizer/Soil Amendment ....

Pests/Weeds/Control ....

....

Watering/Rainfall ....

....

Date Bloomed/Harvested ....

Notes ....

....

....

Rate It: (1) (2) (3) (4) (5)

✿✿✿ PLANT LOG ✿✿✿

PLANT NAME ....

SCIENTIFIC NAME ....
Flower ☐ Vegetable ☐ Fruit ☐ Herb ☐ Shrub ☐ Tree ☐
Annual ☐ Biennial ☐ Perennial ☐ Seedling ☐ Bulb ☐

SUPPLIER .... **COST** ....

Date Germinated.................................... Date Planted...................................

Location .... Sun ☐ Partial Sun ☐ Shade ☐

Fertilizer/Soil Amendment ....

Pests/Weeds/Control ....

....

Watering/Rainfall...

....

Date Bloomed/Harvested ....

Notes ....

....

....

Rate It: (1) (2) (3) (4) (5)

✿✿✿ PLANT LOG ✿✿✿

PLANT NAME ....

SCIENTIFIC NAME ....

Flower ☐ Vegetable ☐ Fruit ☐ Herb ☐ Shrub ☐ Tree ☐

Annual ☐ Biennial ☐ Perennial ☐ Seedling ☐ Bulb ☐

SUPPLIER .... **COST** ....

Date Germinated................................... Date Planted...................................

Location .... Sun ☐ Partial Sun ☐ Shade ☐

Fertilizer/Soil Amendment ....

Pests/Weeds/Control ....

....

Watering/Rainfall...

....

Date Bloomed/Harvested ....

Notes ....

....

....

Rate It: (1) (2) (3) (4) (5)

❧❧❧❧ PLANT LOG ❧❧❧❧

PLANT NAME ....

SCIENTIFIC NAME ....

Flower ☐ Vegetable ☐ Fruit ☐ Herb ☐ Shrub ☐ Tree ☐

Annual ☐ Biennial ☐ Perennial ☐ Seedling ☐ Bulb ☐

SUPPLIER .... **COST** ....

Date Germinated .... Date Planted ....

Location .... Sun ☐ Partial Sun ☐ Shade ☐

Fertilizer/Soil Amendment ....

Pests/Weeds/Control ....

....

Watering/Rainfall ....

....

Date Bloomed/Harvested ....

Notes ....

....

....

Rate It: (1) (2) (3) (4) (5)

~~~~ PLANT LOG ~~~~

PLANT NAME ....

SCIENTIFIC NAME ....

Flower ☐ Vegetable ☐ Fruit ☐ Herb ☐ Shrub ☐ Tree ☐

Annual ☐ Biennial ☐ Perennial ☐ Seedling ☐ Bulb ☐

SUPPLIER .... COST ....

Date Germinated .... Date Planted ....

Location .... Sun ☐ Partial Sun ☐ Shade ☐

Fertilizer/Soil Amendment ....

Pests/Weeds/Control ....

....

Watering/Rainfall ....

....

Date Bloomed/Harvested ....

Notes ....

....

....

Rate It: (1) (2) (3) (4) (5)

~~~ PLANT LOG ~~~

PLANT NAME ....

SCIENTIFIC NAME ....
Flower ☐ Vegetable ☐ Fruit ☐ Herb ☐ Shrub ☐ Tree ☐
Annual ☐ Biennial ☐ Perennial ☐ Seedling ☐ Bulb ☐

SUPPLIER .... **COST** ....

Date Germinated .... Date Planted ....

Location .... Sun ☐ Partial Sun ☐ Shade ☐

Fertilizer/Soil Amendment ....

Pests/Weeds/Control ....

....

Watering/Rainfall...

....

Date Bloomed/Harvested ....

Notes ....

....

....

Rate It: (1)   (2)   (3)   (4)   (5)

≈≈≈ PLANT LOG ≈≈≈

PLANT NAME ....

SCIENTIFIC NAME ....

    Flower ☐ Vegetable ☐ Fruit ☐ Herb ☐ Shrub ☐ Tree ☐

    Annual ☐ Biennial ☐ Perennial ☐ Seedling ☐ Bulb ☐

SUPPLIER .... **COST** ....

Date Germinated.. Date Planted.....................

Location .... Sun ☐ Partial Sun ☐ Shade ☐

Fertilizer/Soil Amendment ....

Pests/Weeds/Control ....

....

Watering/Rainfall..

....

Date Bloomed/Harvested ....

Notes ....

....

....

Rate It: (1) (2) (3) (4) (5)

❧❧❧❧ PLANT LOG ❧❧❧❧

PLANT NAME ....

SCIENTIFIC NAME ....

Flower ☐ Vegetable ☐ Fruit ☐ Herb ☐ Shrub ☐ Tree ☐

Annual ☐ Biennial ☐ Perennial ☐ Seedling ☐ Bulb ☐

SUPPLIER .... **COST** ....

Date Germinated .... Date Planted ....

Location .... Sun ☐ Partial Sun ☐ Shade ☐

Fertilizer/Soil Amendment ....

Pests/Weeds/Control ....

....

Watering/Rainfall ....

....

Date Bloomed/Harvested ....

Notes ....

....

....

Rate It: (1) (2) (3) (4) (5)

✿✿✿ PLANT LOG ✿✿✿

PLANT NAME ....

SCIENTIFIC NAME ....

Flower ☐ Vegetable ☐ Fruit ☐ Herb ☐ Shrub ☐ Tree ☐

Annual ☐ Biennial ☐ Perennial ☐ Seedling ☐ Bulb ☐

SUPPLIER .... COST ....

Date Germinated .... Date Planted ....

Location .... Sun ☐ Partial Sun ☐ Shade ☐

Fertilizer/Soil Amendment ....

Pests/Weeds/Control ....

....

Watering/Rainfall ....

....

Date Bloomed/Harvested ....

Notes ....

....

....

Rate It: (1) (2) (3) (4) (5)

❧ PLANT LOG ❧

PLANT NAME ....

SCIENTIFIC NAME ....

Flower ☐ Vegetable ☐ Fruit ☐ Herb ☐ Shrub ☐ Tree ☐

Annual ☐ Biennial ☐ Perennial ☐ Seedling ☐ Bulb ☐

SUPPLIER .... **COST** ....

Date Germinated .... Date Planted ....

Location .... Sun ☐ Partial Sun ☐ Shade ☐

Fertilizer/Soil Amendment ....

Pests/Weeds/Control ....

....

Watering/Rainfall ....

....

Date Bloomed/Harvested ....

Notes ....

....

....

Rate It: (1) (2) (3) (4) (5)

ꙮꙮ PLANT LOG ꙮꙮ

PLANT NAME ....

SCIENTIFIC NAME ....

Flower ☐ Vegetable ☐ Fruit ☐ Herb ☐ Shrub ☐ Tree ☐

Annual ☐ Biennial ☐ Perennial ☐ Seedling ☐ Bulb ☐

SUPPLIER .... **COST** ....

Date Germinated .... Date Planted ....

Location .... Sun ☐ Partial Sun ☐ Shade ☐

Fertilizer/Soil Amendment ....

Pests/Weeds/Control ....

....

Watering/Rainfall..

....

Date Bloomed/Harvested ....

Notes ....

....

....

Rate It: (1)   (2)   (3)   (4)   (5)

✿✿✿✿✿ PLANT LOG ✿✿✿✿✿

PLANT NAME ....

SCIENTIFIC NAME ....

Flower ☐ Vegetable ☐ Fruit ☐ Herb ☐ Shrub ☐ Tree ☐

Annual ☐ Biennial ☐ Perennial ☐ Seedling ☐ Bulb ☐

SUPPLIER .... **COST** ....

Date Germinated.. Date Planted..

Location .... Sun ☐ Partial Sun ☐ Shade ☐

Fertilizer/Soil Amendment ....

Pests/Weeds/Control ....

....

Watering/Rainfall..

....

Date Bloomed/Harvested ....

Notes ....

....

....

Rate It: (1)   (2)   (3)   (4)   (5)

PLANT LOG

PLANT NAME ....

SCIENTIFIC NAME ....

Flower ☐ Vegetable ☐ Fruit ☐ Herb ☐ Shrub ☐ Tree ☐

Annual ☐ Biennial ☐ Perennial ☐ Seedling ☐ Bulb ☐

SUPPLIER .... **COST** ....

Date Germinated .... Date Planted ....

Location .... Sun ☐ Partial Sun ☐ Shade ☐

Fertilizer/Soil Amendment ....

Pests/Weeds/Control ....

....

Watering/Rainfall ....

....

Date Bloomed/Harvested ....

Notes ....

....

....

Rate It: (1) (2) (3) (4) (5)

PLANT LOG

PLANT NAME ....

SCIENTIFIC NAME ....

Flower ☐ Vegetable ☐ Fruit ☐ Herb ☐ Shrub ☐ Tree ☐

Annual ☐ Biennial ☐ Perennial ☐ Seedling ☐ Bulb ☐

SUPPLIER .... **COST** ....

Date Germinated .... Date Planted ....

Location .... Sun ☐ Partial Sun ☐ Shade ☐

Fertilizer/Soil Amendment ....

Pests/Weeds/Control ....

....

Watering/Rainfall...

....

Date Bloomed/Harvested ....

Notes ....

....

....

Rate It: (1) (2) (3) (4) (5)

❧❧❧ PLANT LOG ❧❧❧

PLANT NAME ....

SCIENTIFIC NAME ....

    Flower ☐ Vegetable ☐ Fruit ☐ Herb ☐ Shrub ☐ Tree ☐

    Annual ☐ Biennial ☐ Perennial ☐ Seedling ☐ Bulb ☐

SUPPLIER .... **COST** ....

Date Germinated .... Date Planted ....

Location .... Sun ☐ Partial Sun ☐ Shade ☐

Fertilizer/Soil Amendment ....

Pests/Weeds/Control ....

....

Watering/Rainfall..

....

Date Bloomed/Harvested ....

Notes ....

....

....

Rate It: (1) (2) (3) (4) (5)

❀❀❀ PLANT LOG ❀❀❀

PLANT NAME ....

SCIENTIFIC NAME ....

Flower ☐ Vegetable ☐ Fruit ☐ Herb ☐ Shrub ☐ Tree ☐

Annual ☐ Biennial ☐ Perennial ☐ Seedling ☐ Bulb ☐

SUPPLIER .... **COST** ....

Date Germinated... Date Planted....................................

Location .... Sun ☐ Partial Sun ☐ Shade ☐

Fertilizer/Soil Amendment ....

Pests/Weeds/Control ....

....

Watering/Rainfall...

....

Date Bloomed/Harvested ....

Notes ....

....

....

Rate It: (1) (2) (3) (4) (5)

✿✿✿ PLANT LOG ✿✿✿

PLANT NAME ....

SCIENTIFIC NAME ....

    Flower ☐ Vegetable ☐ Fruit ☐ Herb ☐ Shrub ☐ Tree ☐

    Annual ☐ Biennial ☐ Perennial ☐ Seedling ☐ Bulb ☐

SUPPLIER .... **COST** ....

Date Germinated .... Date Planted ....

Location .... Sun ☐ Partial Sun ☐ Shade ☐

Fertilizer/Soil Amendment ....

Pests/Weeds/Control ....

....

Watering/Rainfall ....

....

Date Bloomed/Harvested ....

Notes ....

....

....

Rate It: 1   2   3   4   5

~ PLANT LOG ~

PLANT NAME ....

SCIENTIFIC NAME ....

Flower ☐ Vegetable ☐ Fruit ☐ Herb ☐ Shrub ☐ Tree ☐

Annual ☐ Biennial ☐ Perennial ☐ Seedling ☐ Bulb ☐

SUPPLIER .... **COST** ....

Date Germinated .... Date Planted ....

Location .... Sun ☐ Partial Sun ☐ Shade ☐

Fertilizer/Soil Amendment ....

Pests/Weeds/Control ....

....

Watering/Rainfall ....

....

Date Bloomed/Harvested ....

Notes ....

....

....

Rate It: (1) (2) (3) (4) (5)

❧❧❧ PLANT LOG ❧❧❧

PLANT NAME ....

SCIENTIFIC NAME ....

Flower ☐ Vegetable ☐ Fruit ☐ Herb ☐ Shrub ☐ Tree ☐

Annual ☐ Biennial ☐ Perennial ☐ Seedling ☐ Bulb ☐

SUPPLIER .... **COST** ....

Date Germinated .... Date Planted ....

Location .... Sun ☐ Partial Sun ☐ Shade ☐

Fertilizer/Soil Amendment ....

Pests/Weeds/Control ....

....

Watering/Rainfall...

....

Date Bloomed/Harvested ....

Notes ....

....

....

Rate It: (1) (2) (3) (4) (5)

꧁ PLANT LOG ꧁

PLANT NAME ....

SCIENTIFIC NAME ....

Flower ☐ Vegetable ☐ Fruit ☐ Herb ☐ Shrub ☐ Tree ☐

Annual ☐ Biennial ☐ Perennial ☐ Seedling ☐ Bulb ☐

SUPPLIER .... **COST** ....

Date Germinated.................................. Date Planted...........................

Location .... Sun ☐ Partial Sun ☐ Shade ☐

Fertilizer/Soil Amendment ....

Pests/Weeds/Control ....

....

Watering/Rainfall...

....

Date Bloomed/Harvested ....

Notes ....

....

....

Rate It: (1) (2) (3) (4) (5)

⫸⫸ PLANT LOG ⫷⫷

PLANT NAME ....

SCIENTIFIC NAME ....

Flower ☐ Vegetable ☐ Fruit ☐ Herb ☐ Shrub ☐ Tree ☐

Annual ☐ Biennial ☐ Perennial ☐ Seedling ☐ Bulb ☐

SUPPLIER .... **COST** ....

Date Germinated .... Date Planted ....

Location .... Sun ☐ Partial Sun ☐ Shade ☐

Fertilizer/Soil Amendment ....

Pests/Weeds/Control ....

....

Watering/Rainfall...

....

Date Bloomed/Harvested ....

Notes ....

....

....

Rate It: (1) (2) (3) (4) (5)

PLANT LOG

PLANT NAME ....

SCIENTIFIC NAME ....

Flower ☐ Vegetable ☐ Fruit ☐ Herb ☐ Shrub ☐ Tree ☐

Annual ☐ Biennial ☐ Perennial ☐ Seedling ☐ Bulb ☐

SUPPLIER .... COST ....

Date Germinated .... Date Planted ....

Location .... Sun ☐ Partial Sun ☐ Shade ☐

Fertilizer/Soil Amendment ....

Pests/Weeds/Control ....

....

Watering/Rainfall ....

....

Date Bloomed/Harvested ....

Notes ....

....

....

Rate It: (1) (2) (3) (4) (5)

❧❧❧ PLANT LOG ❧❧❧

PLANT NAME ....

SCIENTIFIC NAME ....

Flower ☐ Vegetable ☐ Fruit ☐ Herb ☐ Shrub ☐ Tree ☐

Annual ☐ Biennial ☐ Perennial ☐ Seedling ☐ Bulb ☐

SUPPLIER .... **COST** ....

Date Germinated .... Date Planted ....

Location .... Sun ☐ Partial Sun ☐ Shade ☐

Fertilizer/Soil Amendment ....

Pests/Weeds/Control ....

....

Watering/Rainfall ....

....

Date Bloomed/Harvested ....

Notes ....

....

....

Rate It: (1) (2) (3) (4) (5)

✿✿✿ PLANT LOG ✿✿✿

PLANT NAME ....

SCIENTIFIC NAME ....
Flower ☐ Vegetable ☐ Fruit ☐ Herb ☐ Shrub ☐ Tree ☐
Annual ☐ Biennial ☐ Perennial ☐ Seedling ☐ Bulb ☐

SUPPLIER .... **COST** ....

Date Germinated .... Date Planted ....

Location .... Sun ☐ Partial Sun ☐ Shade ☐

Fertilizer/Soil Amendment ....

Pests/Weeds/Control ....

....

Watering/Rainfall ....

....

Date Bloomed/Harvested ....

Notes ....

....

....

Rate It: (1) (2) (3) (4) (5)

~~~~~~ PLANT LOG ~~~~~~

PLANT NAME ....

SCIENTIFIC NAME ....

    Flower ☐ Vegetable ☐ Fruit ☐ Herb ☐ Shrub ☐ Tree ☐

    Annual ☐ Biennial ☐ Perennial ☐ Seedling ☐ Bulb ☐

SUPPLIER .... **COST** ....

Date Germinated .... Date Planted ....

Location .... Sun ☐ Partial Sun ☐ Shade ☐

Fertilizer/Soil Amendment ....

Pests/Weeds/Control ....

....

Watering/Rainfall..

....

Date Bloomed/Harvested ....

Notes ....

....

....

Rate It: (1)   (2)   (3)   (4)   (5)

✿✿✿ PLANT LOG ✿✿✿

PLANT NAME ....

SCIENTIFIC NAME ....
  Flower ☐ Vegetable ☐ Fruit ☐ Herb ☐ Shrub ☐ Tree ☐
  Annual ☐ Biennial ☐ Perennial ☐ Seedling ☐ Bulb ☐

SUPPLIER .... **COST** ....

Date Germinated .... Date Planted ....

Location .... Sun ☐ Partial Sun ☐ Shade ☐

Fertilizer/Soil Amendment ....

Pests/Weeds/Control ....

....

Watering/Rainfall ....

....

Date Bloomed/Harvested ....

Notes ....

....

....

Rate It: (1)   (2)   (3)   (4)   (5)

🌿 PLANT LOG 🌿

PLANT NAME ....

SCIENTIFIC NAME ....

Flower ☐   Vegetable ☐   Fruit ☐   Herb ☐   Shrub ☐   Tree ☐

Annual ☐   Biennial ☐   Perennial ☐   Seedling ☐   Bulb ☐

SUPPLIER .... **COST** ....

Date Germinated................................ Date Planted ....

Location .... Sun ☐   Partial Sun ☐   Shade ☐

Fertilizer/Soil Amendment ....

Pests/Weeds/Control ....

....

Watering/Rainfall...

....

Date Bloomed/Harvested ....

Notes ....

....

....

Rate It: (1)   (2)   (3)   (4)   (5)

ꙮꙮꙮ PLANT LOG ꙮꙮꙮ

PLANT NAME ....

SCIENTIFIC NAME ....

Flower ☐ Vegetable ☐ Fruit ☐ Herb ☐ Shrub ☐ Tree ☐

Annual ☐ Biennial ☐ Perennial ☐ Seedling ☐ Bulb ☐

SUPPLIER .... **COST** ....

Date Germinated .... Date Planted ....

Location .... Sun ☐ Partial Sun ☐ Shade ☐

Fertilizer/Soil Amendment ....

Pests/Weeds/Control ....

....

Watering/Rainfall..

....

Date Bloomed/Harvested ....

Notes ....

....

....

Rate It: (1) (2) (3) (4) (5)

PLANT LOG

PLANT NAME ....

SCIENTIFIC NAME ....

Flower ☐ Vegetable ☐ Fruit ☐ Herb ☐ Shrub ☐ Tree ☐

Annual ☐ Biennial ☐ Perennial ☐ Seedling ☐ Bulb ☐

SUPPLIER .... **COST** ....

Date Germinated .... Date Planted ....

Location .... Sun ☐ Partial Sun ☐ Shade ☐

Fertilizer/Soil Amendment ....

Pests/Weeds/Control ....

....

Watering/Rainfall ....

....

Date Bloomed/Harvested ....

Notes ....

....

....

Rate It: (1) (2) (3) (4) (5)

✿✿✿✿ PLANT LOG ✿✿✿✿

PLANT NAME ....

SCIENTIFIC NAME ....

Flower ☐ Vegetable ☐ Fruit ☐ Herb ☐ Shrub ☐ Tree ☐

Annual ☐ Biennial ☐ Perennial ☐ Seedling ☐ Bulb ☐

SUPPLIER .... **COST** ....

Date Germinated .... Date Planted ....

Location .... Sun ☐ Partial Sun ☐ Shade ☐

Fertilizer/Soil Amendment ....

Pests/Weeds/Control ....

....

Watering/Rainfall ....

....

Date Bloomed/Harvested ....

Notes ....

....

....

Rate It: (1) (2) (3) (4) (5)

❧❧❧ PLANT LOG ❧❧❧

PLANT NAME ....

SCIENTIFIC NAME ....

Flower ☐ Vegetable ☐ Fruit ☐ Herb ☐ Shrub ☐ Tree ☐

Annual ☐ Biennial ☐ Perennial ☐ Seedling ☐ Bulb ☐

SUPPLIER .... **COST** ....

Date Germinated .... Date Planted ....

Location .... Sun ☐ Partial Sun ☐ Shade ☐

Fertilizer/Soil Amendment ....

Pests/Weeds/Control ....

....

Watering/Rainfall ....

....

Date Bloomed/Harvested ....

Notes ....

....

....

Rate It: (1) (2) (3) (4) (5)

✿✿✿ PLANT LOG ✿✿✿

PLANT NAME ....

SCIENTIFIC NAME ....

Flower ☐ Vegetable ☐ Fruit ☐ Herb ☐ Shrub ☐ Tree ☐

Annual ☐ Biennial ☐ Perennial ☐ Seedling ☐ Bulb ☐

SUPPLIER .... **COST** ....

Date Germinated .... Date Planted ....

Location .... Sun ☐ Partial Sun ☐ Shade ☐

Fertilizer/Soil Amendment ....

Pests/Weeds/Control ....

....

Watering/Rainfall ....

....

Date Bloomed/Harvested ....

Notes ....

....

....

Rate It: (1)   (2)   (3)   (4)   (5)

❧❧❧ PLANT LOG ❧❧❧

PLANT NAME ....

SCIENTIFIC NAME ....

Flower ☐ Vegetable ☐ Fruit ☐ Herb ☐ Shrub ☐ Tree ☐

Annual ☐ Biennial ☐ Perennial ☐ Seedling ☐ Bulb ☐

SUPPLIER .... **COST** ....

Date Germinated .... Date Planted ....

Location .... Sun ☐ Partial Sun ☐ Shade ☐

Fertilizer/Soil Amendment ....

Pests/Weeds/Control ....

....

Watering/Rainfall ....

....

Date Bloomed/Harvested ....

Notes ....

....

....

Rate It: (1) (2) (3) (4) (5)

〰〰 PLANT LOG 〰〰

PLANT NAME ....

SCIENTIFIC NAME ....

Flower ☐ Vegetable ☐ Fruit ☐ Herb ☐ Shrub ☐ Tree ☐

Annual ☐ Biennial ☐ Perennial ☐ Seedling ☐ Bulb ☐

SUPPLIER .... **COST** ....

Date Germinated.. Date Planted...........................

Location .... Sun ☐ Partial Sun ☐ Shade ☐

Fertilizer/Soil Amendment ....

Pests/Weeds/Control ....

....

Watering/Rainfall..

....

Date Bloomed/Harvested ....

Notes ....

....

....

Rate It: (1) (2) (3) (4) (5)

✿ PLANT LOG ✿

PLANT NAME ....

SCIENTIFIC NAME ....

Flower ☐ Vegetable ☐ Fruit ☐ Herb ☐ Shrub ☐ Tree ☐

Annual ☐ Biennial ☐ Perennial ☐ Seedling ☐ Bulb ☐

SUPPLIER .... **COST** ....

Date Germinated .... Date Planted ....

Location .... Sun ☐ Partial Sun ☐ Shade ☐

Fertilizer/Soil Amendment ....

Pests/Weeds/Control ....

....

Watering/Rainfall...

....

Date Bloomed/Harvested ....

Notes ....

....

....

Rate It: (1)   (2)   (3)   (4)   (5)

✿✿✿✿ PLANT LOG ✿✿✿✿

PLANT NAME ....

SCIENTIFIC NAME ....

Flower ☐ Vegetable ☐ Fruit ☐ Herb ☐ Shrub ☐ Tree ☐

Annual ☐ Biennial ☐ Perennial ☐ Seedling ☐ Bulb ☐

SUPPLIER .... **COST** ....

Date Germinated .... Date Planted ....

Location .... Sun ☐ Partial Sun ☐ Shade ☐

Fertilizer/Soil Amendment ....

Pests/Weeds/Control ....

....

Watering/Rainfall ....

....

Date Bloomed/Harvested ....

Notes ....

....

....

Rate It: (1)   (2)   (3)   (4)   (5)

✿✿✿✿✿ PLANT LOG ✿✿✿✿✿

PLANT NAME ....

SCIENTIFIC NAME ....

Flower ☐ Vegetable ☐ Fruit ☐ Herb ☐ Shrub ☐ Tree ☐

Annual ☐ Biennial ☐ Perennial ☐ Seedling ☐ Bulb ☐

SUPPLIER .... **COST** ....

Date Germinated .... Date Planted ....

Location .... Sun ☐ Partial Sun ☐ Shade ☐

Fertilizer/Soil Amendment ....

Pests/Weeds/Control ....

....

Watering/Rainfall ....

....

Date Bloomed/Harvested ....

Notes ....

....

....

Rate It: (1) (2) (3) (4) (5)

✿✿✿ PLANT LOG ✿✿✿

PLANT NAME ....

SCIENTIFIC NAME ....

Flower ☐ Vegetable ☐ Fruit ☐ Herb ☐ Shrub ☐ Tree ☐

Annual ☐ Biennial ☐ Perennial ☐ Seedling ☐ Bulb ☐

SUPPLIER .... **COST** ....

Date Germinated .... Date Planted ....

Location .... Sun ☐ Partial Sun ☐ Shade ☐

Fertilizer/Soil Amendment ....

Pests/Weeds/Control ....

....

Watering/Rainfall ....

....

Date Bloomed/Harvested ....

Notes ....

....

....

Rate It: (1) (2) (3) (4) (5)

~≈≈≈≈~ PLANT LOG ~≈≈≈≈~

PLANT NAME ....

SCIENTIFIC NAME ....

Flower ☐ Vegetable ☐ Fruit ☐ Herb ☐ Shrub ☐ Tree ☐

Annual ☐ Biennial ☐ Perennial ☐ Seedling ☐ Bulb ☐

SUPPLIER .... **COST** ....

Date Germinated.. Date Planted...................................

Location .... Sun ☐ Partial Sun ☐ Shade ☐

Fertilizer/Soil Amendment ....

Pests/Weeds/Control ....

....

Watering/Rainfall..

....

Date Bloomed/Harvested ....

Notes ....

....

....

Rate It: (1) (2) (3) (4) (5)

PLANT LOG

PLANT NAME ....

SCIENTIFIC NAME ....

Flower ☐ Vegetable ☐ Fruit ☐ Herb ☐ Shrub ☐ Tree ☐

Annual ☐ Biennial ☐ Perennial ☐ Seedling ☐ Bulb ☐

SUPPLIER .... **COST** ....

Date Germinated .... Date Planted ....

Location .... Sun ☐ Partial Sun ☐ Shade ☐

Fertilizer/Soil Amendment ....

Pests/Weeds/Control ....

....

Watering/Rainfall ....

....

Date Bloomed/Harvested ....

Notes ....

....

....

Rate It: (1) (2) (3) (4) (5)

✺✺✺ PLANT LOG ✺✺✺

PLANT NAME ....

SCIENTIFIC NAME ....

Flower ☐ Vegetable ☐ Fruit ☐ Herb ☐ Shrub ☐ Tree ☐

Annual ☐ Biennial ☐ Perennial ☐ Seedling ☐ Bulb ☐

SUPPLIER .... **COST** ....

Date Germinated......................... Date Planted.....................

Location .... Sun ☐ Partial Sun ☐ Shade ☐

Fertilizer/Soil Amendment ....

Pests/Weeds/Control ....

....

Watering/Rainfall..

....

Date Bloomed/Harvested ....

Notes ....

....

....

Rate It: (1) (2) (3) (4) (5)

꧁ PLANT LOG ꧂

PLANT NAME ....

SCIENTIFIC NAME ....

Flower ☐ Vegetable ☐ Fruit ☐ Herb ☐ Shrub ☐ Tree ☐

Annual ☐ Biennial ☐ Perennial ☐ Seedling ☐ Bulb ☐

SUPPLIER .... **COST** ....

Date Germinated .... Date Planted ....

Location .... Sun ☐ Partial Sun ☐ Shade ☐

Fertilizer/Soil Amendment ....

Pests/Weeds/Control ....

....

Watering/Rainfall ....

....

Date Bloomed/Harvested ....

Notes ....

....

....

Rate It: (1) (2) (3) (4) (5)

✿✿✿ PLANT LOG ✿✿✿

PLANT NAME ....

SCIENTIFIC NAME ....

Flower ☐ Vegetable ☐ Fruit ☐ Herb ☐ Shrub ☐ Tree ☐

Annual ☐ Biennial ☐ Perennial ☐ Seedling ☐ Bulb ☐

SUPPLIER .... **COST** ....

Date Germinated .... Date Planted ....

Location .... Sun ☐ Partial Sun ☐ Shade ☐

Fertilizer/Soil Amendment ....

Pests/Weeds/Control ....

....

Watering/Rainfall ....

....

Date Bloomed/Harvested ....

Notes ....

....

....

Rate It: (1) (2) (3) (4) (5)

✿✿✿ PLANT LOG ✿✿✿

PLANT NAME ....

SCIENTIFIC NAME ....

Flower ☐ Vegetable ☐ Fruit ☐ Herb ☐ Shrub ☐ Tree ☐

Annual ☐ Biennial ☐ Perennial ☐ Seedling ☐ Bulb ☐

SUPPLIER .... **COST** ....

Date Germinated .... Date Planted ....

Location .... Sun ☐ Partial Sun ☐ Shade ☐

Fertilizer/Soil Amendment ....

Pests/Weeds/Control ....

....

Watering/Rainfall...

....

Date Bloomed/Harvested ....

Notes ....

....

....

Rate It: (1) (2) (3) (4) (5)

🌿 PLANT LOG 🌿

PLANT NAME ....

SCIENTIFIC NAME ....

Flower ☐ Vegetable ☐ Fruit ☐ Herb ☐ Shrub ☐ Tree ☐

Annual ☐ Biennial ☐ Perennial ☐ Seedling ☐ Bulb ☐

SUPPLIER .... **COST** ....

Date Germinated .... Date Planted ....

Location .... Sun ☐ Partial Sun ☐ Shade ☐

Fertilizer/Soil Amendment ....

Pests/Weeds/Control ....

....

Watering/Rainfall ....

....

Date Bloomed/Harvested ....

Notes ....

....

....

Rate It: (1) (2) (3) (4) (5)

✿✿✿✿ PLANT LOG ✿✿✿✿

PLANT NAME ....

SCIENTIFIC NAME ....

Flower ☐ Vegetable ☐ Fruit ☐ Herb ☐ Shrub ☐ Tree ☐

Annual ☐ Biennial ☐ Perennial ☐ Seedling ☐ Bulb ☐

SUPPLIER .... **COST** ....

Date Germinated .... Date Planted ....

Location .... Sun ☐ Partial Sun ☐ Shade ☐

Fertilizer/Soil Amendment ....

Pests/Weeds/Control ....

....

Watering/Rainfall ....

....

Date Bloomed/Harvested ....

Notes ....

....

....

Rate It: (1) (2) (3) (4) (5)

✺✺✺ PLANT LOG ✺✺✺

PLANT NAME ....

SCIENTIFIC NAME ....

     Flower ☐ Vegetable ☐ Fruit ☐ Herb ☐ Shrub ☐ Tree ☐

     Annual ☐ Biennial ☐ Perennial ☐ Seedling ☐ Bulb ☐

SUPPLIER .... **COST** ....

Date Germinated .... Date Planted ....

Location .... Sun ☐ Partial Sun ☐ Shade ☐

Fertilizer/Soil Amendment ....

Pests/Weeds/Control ....

....

Watering/Rainfall ....

....

Date Bloomed/Harvested ....

Notes ....

....

....

Rate It: (1) (2) (3) (4) (5)

~~~~~ PLANT LOG ~~~~~

PLANT NAME ....

SCIENTIFIC NAME ....

Flower ☐ Vegetable ☐ Fruit ☐ Herb ☐ Shrub ☐ Tree ☐

Annual ☐ Biennial ☐ Perennial ☐ Seedling ☐ Bulb ☐

SUPPLIER .... **COST** ....

Date Germinated .... Date Planted ....

Location .... Sun ☐ Partial Sun ☐ Shade ☐

Fertilizer/Soil Amendment ....

Pests/Weeds/Control ....

....

Watering/Rainfall ....

....

Date Bloomed/Harvested ....

Notes ....

....

....

Rate It: (1) (2) (3) (4) (5)

❧❧❧ PLANT LOG ❧❧❧

PLANT NAME ....

SCIENTIFIC NAME ....

Flower ☐ Vegetable ☐ Fruit ☐ Herb ☐ Shrub ☐ Tree ☐

Annual ☐ Biennial ☐ Perennial ☐ Seedling ☐ Bulb ☐

SUPPLIER .... **COST** ....

Date Germinated .... Date Planted ....

Location .... Sun ☐ Partial Sun ☐ Shade ☐

Fertilizer/Soil Amendment ....

Pests/Weeds/Control ....

....

Watering/Rainfall ....

....

Date Bloomed/Harvested ....

Notes ....

....

....

Rate It: (1) (2) (3) (4) (5)

✿✿✿✿ PLANT LOG ✿✿✿✿

PLANT NAME ....

SCIENTIFIC NAME ....

Flower ☐ Vegetable ☐ Fruit ☐ Herb ☐ Shrub ☐ Tree ☐

Annual ☐ Biennial ☐ Perennial ☐ Seedling ☐ Bulb ☐

SUPPLIER .... **COST** ....

Date Germinated .... Date Planted ....

Location .... Sun ☐ Partial Sun ☐ Shade ☐

Fertilizer/Soil Amendment ....

Pests/Weeds/Control ....

....

Watering/Rainfall...

....

Date Bloomed/Harvested ....

Notes ....

....

....

Rate It: (1) (2) (3) (4) (5)

❧ PLANT LOG ❧

PLANT NAME ....

SCIENTIFIC NAME ....

Flower ☐ Vegetable ☐ Fruit ☐ Herb ☐ Shrub ☐ Tree ☐

Annual ☐ Biennial ☐ Perennial ☐ Seedling ☐ Bulb ☐

SUPPLIER .... **COST** ....

Date Germinated .... Date Planted ....

Location .... Sun ☐ Partial Sun ☐ Shade ☐

Fertilizer/Soil Amendment ....

Pests/Weeds/Control ....

....

Watering/Rainfall ....

....

Date Bloomed/Harvested ....

Notes ....

....

....

Rate It: (1)   (2)   (3)   (4)   (5)

PLANT LOG

PLANT NAME ....

SCIENTIFIC NAME ....

Flower ☐ Vegetable ☐ Fruit ☐ Herb ☐ Shrub ☐ Tree ☐

Annual ☐ Biennial ☐ Perennial ☐ Seedling ☐ Bulb ☐

SUPPLIER .... **COST** ....

Date Germinated .... Date Planted ....

Location .... Sun ☐ Partial Sun ☐ Shade ☐

Fertilizer/Soil Amendment ....

Pests/Weeds/Control ....

....

Watering/Rainfall ....

....

Date Bloomed/Harvested ....

Notes ....

....

....

Rate It: ① ② ③ ④ ⑤

·❧ PLANT LOG ❧·

PLANT NAME ....

SCIENTIFIC NAME ....

    Flower ☐ Vegetable ☐ Fruit ☐ Herb ☐ Shrub ☐ Tree ☐

    Annual ☐ Biennial ☐ Perennial ☐ Seedling ☐ Bulb ☐

SUPPLIER .... **COST** ....

Date Germinated .... Date Planted ....

Location .... Sun ☐ Partial Sun ☐ Shade ☐

Fertilizer/Soil Amendment ....

Pests/Weeds/Control ....

....

Watering/Rainfall ....

....

Date Bloomed/Harvested ....

Notes ....

....

....

Rate It: (1) (2) (3) (4) (5)

✿✿✿✿✿ PLANT LOG ✿✿✿✿✿

PLANT NAME ....

SCIENTIFIC NAME ....

Flower ☐ Vegetable ☐ Fruit ☐ Herb ☐ Shrub ☐ Tree ☐

Annual ☐ Biennial ☐ Perennial ☐ Seedling ☐ Bulb ☐

SUPPLIER .... **COST** ....

Date Germinated................................... Date Planted ....

Location .... Sun ☐ Partial Sun ☐ Shade ☐

Fertilizer/Soil Amendment ....

Pests/Weeds/Control ....

....

Watering/Rainfall...

....

Date Bloomed/Harvested ....

Notes ....

....

....

Rate It: (1) (2) (3) (4) (5)

✿✿✿ PLANT LOG ✿✿✿

PLANT NAME ....

SCIENTIFIC NAME ....

   Flower ☐   Vegetable ☐   Fruit ☐   Herb ☐   Shrub ☐   Tree ☐

   Annual ☐   Biennial ☐   Perennial ☐   Seedling ☐   Bulb ☐

SUPPLIER .... **COST** ....

Date Germinated .... Date Planted ....

Location .... Sun ☐   Partial Sun ☐   Shade ☐

Fertilizer/Soil Amendment ....

Pests/Weeds/Control ....

....

Watering/Rainfall ....

....

Date Bloomed/Harvested ....

Notes ....

....

....

Rate It: (1)   (2)   (3)   (4)   (5)

~ PLANT LOG ~

PLANT NAME ....

SCIENTIFIC NAME ....
    Flower ☐ Vegetable ☐ Fruit ☐ Herb ☐ Shrub ☐ Tree ☐
    Annual ☐ Biennial ☐ Perennial ☐ Seedling ☐ Bulb ☐

SUPPLIER .... **COST** ....

Date Germinated .... Date Planted ....

Location .... Sun ☐ Partial Sun ☐ Shade ☐

Fertilizer/Soil Amendment ....

Pests/Weeds/Control ....

....

Watering/Rainfall ....

....

Date Bloomed/Harvested ....

Notes ....

....

....

Rate It: (1) (2) (3) (4) (5)

✤✤✤ PLANT LOG ✤✤✤

PLANT NAME ....

SCIENTIFIC NAME ....

    Flower ☐   Vegetable ☐   Fruit ☐   Herb ☐   Shrub ☐   Tree ☐

    Annual ☐   Biennial ☐   Perennial ☐   Seedling ☐   Bulb ☐

SUPPLIER .... **COST** ....

Date Germinated .... Date Planted ....

Location .... Sun ☐   Partial Sun ☐   Shade ☐

Fertilizer/Soil Amendment ....

Pests/Weeds/Control ....

....

Watering/Rainfall...

....

Date Bloomed/Harvested ....

Notes ....

....

....

Rate It: (1)   (2)   (3)   (4)   (5)

✿✿✿✿ PLANT LOG ✿✿✿✿

PLANT NAME ....

SCIENTIFIC NAME ....

Flower ☐ Vegetable ☐ Fruit ☐ Herb ☐ Shrub ☐ Tree ☐

Annual ☐ Biennial ☐ Perennial ☐ Seedling ☐ Bulb ☐

SUPPLIER .... **COST** ....

Date Germinated .... Date Planted ....

Location .... Sun ☐ Partial Sun ☐ Shade ☐

Fertilizer/Soil Amendment ....

Pests/Weeds/Control ....

....

Watering/Rainfall ....

....

Date Bloomed/Harvested ....

Notes ....

....

....

Rate It: (1) (2) (3) (4) (5)

PLANT LOG

PLANT NAME ....

SCIENTIFIC NAME ....

    Flower ☐ Vegetable ☐ Fruit ☐ Herb ☐ Shrub ☐ Tree ☐

    Annual ☐ Biennial ☐ Perennial ☐ Seedling ☐ Bulb ☐

SUPPLIER .... **COST** ....

Date Germinated .... Date Planted ....

Location .... Sun ☐ Partial Sun ☐ Shade ☐

Fertilizer/Soil Amendment ....

Pests/Weeds/Control ....

....

Watering/Rainfall ....

....

Date Bloomed/Harvested ....

Notes ....

....

....

Rate It: (1) (2) (3) (4) (5)

✿✿✿ PLANT LOG ✿✿✿

PLANT NAME ....

SCIENTIFIC NAME ....

Flower ☐ Vegetable ☐ Fruit ☐ Herb ☐ Shrub ☐ Tree ☐

Annual ☐ Biennial ☐ Perennial ☐ Seedling ☐ Bulb ☐

SUPPLIER .... **COST** ....

Date Germinated .... Date Planted ....

Location .... Sun ☐ Partial Sun ☐ Shade ☐

Fertilizer/Soil Amendment ....

Pests/Weeds/Control ....

....

Watering/Rainfall ....

....

Date Bloomed/Harvested ....

Notes ....

....

....

Rate It: (1)　(2)　(3)　(4)　(5)

❧ PLANT LOG ❧

PLANT NAME ....

SCIENTIFIC NAME ....

Flower ☐ Vegetable ☐ Fruit ☐ Herb ☐ Shrub ☐ Tree ☐

Annual ☐ Biennial ☐ Perennial ☐ Seedling ☐ Bulb ☐

SUPPLIER .... COST ....

Date Germinated .... Date Planted ....

Location .... Sun ☐ Partial Sun ☐ Shade ☐

Fertilizer/Soil Amendment ....

Pests/Weeds/Control ....

....

Watering/Rainfall ....

....

Date Bloomed/Harvested ....

Notes ....

....

....

Rate It: (1) (2) (3) (4) (5)

PLANT LOG

PLANT NAME ....

SCIENTIFIC NAME ....

Flower ☐ Vegetable ☐ Fruit ☐ Herb ☐ Shrub ☐ Tree ☐

Annual ☐ Biennial ☐ Perennial ☐ Seedling ☐ Bulb ☐

SUPPLIER .... **COST** ....

Date Germinated .... Date Planted ....

Location .... Sun ☐ Partial Sun ☐ Shade ☐

Fertilizer/Soil Amendment ....

Pests/Weeds/Control ....

....

Watering/Rainfall ....

....

Date Bloomed/Harvested ....

Notes ....

....

....

Rate It: (1) (2) (3) (4) (5)

✧✧✧✧ PLANT LOG ✧✧✧✧

PLANT NAME ....

SCIENTIFIC NAME ....

Flower ☐ Vegetable ☐ Fruit ☐ Herb ☐ Shrub ☐ Tree ☐

Annual ☐ Biennial ☐ Perennial ☐ Seedling ☐ Bulb ☐

SUPPLIER .... **COST** ....

Date Germinated .... Date Planted ....

Location .... Sun ☐ Partial Sun ☐ Shade ☐

Fertilizer/Soil Amendment ....

Pests/Weeds/Control ....

....

Watering/Rainfall ....

....

Date Bloomed/Harvested ....

Notes ....

....

....

Rate It: 1 2 3 4 5

❧❧❧ PLANT LOG ❧❧❧

PLANT NAME

SCIENTIFIC NAME

Flower ☐ Vegetable ☐ Fruit ☐ Herb ☐ Shrub ☐ Tree ☐

Annual ☐ Biennial ☐ Perennial ☐ Seedling ☐ Bulb ☐

SUPPLIER .... **COST**

Date Germinated .... Date Planted ....

Location .... Sun ☐ Partial Sun ☐ Shade ☐

Fertilizer/Soil Amendment ....

Pests/Weeds/Control ....

....

Watering/Rainfall....................................

....

Date Bloomed/Harvested ....

Notes ....

....

....

Rate It: (1) (2) (3) (4) (5)

~ PLANT LOG ~

PLANT NAME ....

SCIENTIFIC NAME ....

Flower ☐ Vegetable ☐ Fruit ☐ Herb ☐ Shrub ☐ Tree ☐

Annual ☐ Biennial ☐ Perennial ☐ Seedling ☐ Bulb ☐

SUPPLIER .... **COST** ....

Date Germinated .... Date Planted ....

Location .... Sun ☐ Partial Sun ☐ Shade ☐

Fertilizer/Soil Amendment ....

Pests/Weeds/Control ....

....

Watering/Rainfall ....

....

Date Bloomed/Harvested ....

Notes ....

....

....

Rate It:

❧ PLANT LOG ❧

PLANT NAME ....

SCIENTIFIC NAME ....

Flower ☐ Vegetable ☐ Fruit ☐ Herb ☐ Shrub ☐ Tree ☐

Annual ☐ Biennial ☐ Perennial ☐ Seedling ☐ Bulb ☐

SUPPLIER .... **COST** ....

Date Germinated.................................Date Planted.....................

Location .... Sun ☐ Partial Sun ☐ Shade ☐

Fertilizer/Soil Amendment ....

Pests/Weeds/Control ....

....

Watering/Rainfall...

....

Date Bloomed/Harvested ....

Notes ....

....

....

Rate It: (1) (2) (3) (4) (5)

✤✤✤ PLANT LOG ✤✤✤

PLANT NAME ....

SCIENTIFIC NAME ....

Flower ☐ Vegetable ☐ Fruit ☐ Herb ☐ Shrub ☐ Tree ☐

Annual ☐ Biennial ☐ Perennial ☐ Seedling ☐ Bulb ☐

SUPPLIER .... **COST** ....

Date Germinated .... Date Planted ....

Location .... Sun ☐ Partial Sun ☐ Shade ☐

Fertilizer/Soil Amendment ....

Pests/Weeds/Control ....

....

Watering/Rainfall ....

....

Date Bloomed/Harvested ....

Notes ....

....

....

Rate It: (1) (2) (3) (4) (5)

꧁ PLANT LOG ꧂

PLANT NAME ....

SCIENTIFIC NAME ....

Flower ☐ Vegetable ☐ Fruit ☐ Herb ☐ Shrub ☐ Tree ☐

Annual ☐ Biennial ☐ Perennial ☐ Seedling ☐ Bulb ☐

SUPPLIER .... **COST** ....

Date Germinated .... Date Planted ....

Location .... Sun ☐ Partial Sun ☐ Shade ☐

Fertilizer/Soil Amendment ....

Pests/Weeds/Control ....

....

Watering/Rainfall...

....

Date Bloomed/Harvested ....

Notes ....

....

....

Rate It: (1) (2) (3) (4) (5)

·⁓⁓⁓· PLANT LOG ·⁓⁓⁓·

PLANT NAME

SCIENTIFIC NAME

Flower ☐ Vegetable ☐ Fruit ☐ Herb ☐ Shrub ☐ Tree ☐

Annual ☐ Biennial ☐ Perennial ☐ Seedling ☐ Bulb ☐

SUPPLIER **COST**

Date Germinated Date Planted

Location Sun ☐ Partial Sun ☐ Shade ☐

Fertilizer/Soil Amendment

Pests/Weeds/Control

Watering/Rainfall

Date Bloomed/Harvested

Notes

Rate It: (1) (2) (3) (4) (5)

✿✿✿✿✿ PLANT LOG ✿✿✿✿✿

PLANT NAME ....

SCIENTIFIC NAME ....

Flower ☐ Vegetable ☐ Fruit ☐ Herb ☐ Shrub ☐ Tree ☐

Annual ☐ Biennial ☐ Perennial ☐ Seedling ☐ Bulb ☐

SUPPLIER .... **COST** ....

Date Germinated .... Date Planted ....

Location .... Sun ☐ Partial Sun ☐ Shade ☐

Fertilizer/Soil Amendment ....

Pests/Weeds/Control ....

....

Watering/Rainfall ....

....

Date Bloomed/Harvested ....

Notes ....

....

....

Rate It: (1)   (2)   (3)   (4)   (5)

༺ PLANT LOG ༻

PLANT NAME ....

SCIENTIFIC NAME ....

Flower ☐ Vegetable ☐ Fruit ☐ Herb ☐ Shrub ☐ Tree ☐

Annual ☐ Biennial ☐ Perennial ☐ Seedling ☐ Bulb ☐

SUPPLIER .... **COST** ....

Date Germinated .... Date Planted ....

Location .... Sun ☐ Partial Sun ☐ Shade ☐

Fertilizer/Soil Amendment ....

Pests/Weeds/Control ....

....

Watering/Rainfall ....

....

Date Bloomed/Harvested ....

Notes ....

....

....

Rate It: (1)   (2)   (3)   (4)   (5)

✿✿✿ PLANT LOG ✿✿✿

PLANT NAME ....

SCIENTIFIC NAME ....

Flower ☐ Vegetable ☐ Fruit ☐ Herb ☐ Shrub ☐ Tree ☐

Annual ☐ Biennial ☐ Perennial ☐ Seedling ☐ Bulb ☐

SUPPLIER .... **COST** ....

Date Germinated .... Date Planted ....

Location .... Sun ☐ Partial Sun ☐ Shade ☐

Fertilizer/Soil Amendment ....

Pests/Weeds/Control ....

....

Watering/Rainfall ....

....

Date Bloomed/Harvested ....

Notes ....

....

....

Rate It: (1) (2) (3) (4) (5)

✿✿✿ PLANT LOG ✿✿✿

PLANT NAME ....

SCIENTIFIC NAME ....

Flower ☐ Vegetable ☐ Fruit ☐ Herb ☐ Shrub ☐ Tree ☐

Annual ☐ Biennial ☐ Perennial ☐ Seedling ☐ Bulb ☐

SUPPLIER .... **COST** ....

Date Germinated................................Date Planted.....................

Location .... Sun ☐ Partial Sun ☐ Shade ☐

Fertilizer/Soil Amendment ....

Pests/Weeds/Control ....

....

Watering/Rainfall..

....

Date Bloomed/Harvested ....

Notes ....

....

....

Rate It: (1) (2) (3) (4) (5)

❧❧ PLANT LOG ❧❧

PLANT NAME ....

SCIENTIFIC NAME ....

Flower ☐ Vegetable ☐ Fruit ☐ Herb ☐ Shrub ☐ Tree ☐

Annual ☐ Biennial ☐ Perennial ☐ Seedling ☐ Bulb ☐

SUPPLIER .... **COST** ....

Date Germinated .... Date Planted ....

Location .... Sun ☐ Partial Sun ☐ Shade ☐

Fertilizer/Soil Amendment ....

Pests/Weeds/Control ....

....

Watering/Rainfall..

....

Date Bloomed/Harvested ....

Notes ....

....

....

Rate It: (1)   (2)   (3)   (4)   (5)

~ PLANT LOG ~

PLANT NAME ....

SCIENTIFIC NAME ....

    Flower ☐   Vegetable ☐   Fruit ☐   Herb ☐   Shrub ☐   Tree ☐

    Annual ☐   Biennial ☐   Perennial ☐   Seedling ☐   Bulb ☐

SUPPLIER .... **COST** ....

Date Germinated .... Date Planted ....

Location .... Sun ☐   Partial Sun ☐   Shade ☐

Fertilizer/Soil Amendment ....

Pests/Weeds/Control ....

....

Watering/Rainfall ....

....

Date Bloomed/Harvested ....

Notes ....

....

....

Rate It: (1)   (2)   (3)   (4)   (5)

✿✿✿ PLANT LOG ✿✿✿

PLANT NAME ....

SCIENTIFIC NAME ....

Flower ☐ Vegetable ☐ Fruit ☐ Herb ☐ Shrub ☐ Tree ☐

Annual ☐ Biennial ☐ Perennial ☐ Seedling ☐ Bulb ☐

SUPPLIER .... **COST** ....

Date Germinated .... Date Planted ....

Location .... Sun ☐ Partial Sun ☐ Shade ☐

Fertilizer/Soil Amendment ....

Pests/Weeds/Control ....

....

Watering/Rainfall ....

....

Date Bloomed/Harvested ....

Notes ....

....

....

Rate It: (1) (2) (3) (4) (5)

✿✿✿ PLANT LOG ✿✿✿

PLANT NAME ....

SCIENTIFIC NAME ....

Flower ☐ Vegetable ☐ Fruit ☐ Herb ☐ Shrub ☐ Tree ☐

Annual ☐ Biennial ☐ Perennial ☐ Seedling ☐ Bulb ☐

SUPPLIER .... **COST** ....

Date Germinated .... Date Planted ....

Location .... Sun ☐ Partial Sun ☐ Shade ☐

Fertilizer/Soil Amendment ....

Pests/Weeds/Control ....

....

Watering/Rainfall ....

....

Date Bloomed/Harvested ....

Notes ....

....

....

Rate It:

✿✿✿ PLANT LOG ✿✿✿

PLANT NAME ....

SCIENTIFIC NAME ....

Flower ☐ Vegetable ☐ Fruit ☐ Herb ☐ Shrub ☐ Tree ☐

Annual ☐ Biennial ☐ Perennial ☐ Seedling ☐ Bulb ☐

SUPPLIER .... **COST** ....

Date Germinated.................................... Date Planted...................

Location .... Sun ☐ Partial Sun ☐ Shade ☐

Fertilizer/Soil Amendment ....

Pests/Weeds/Control ....

....

Watering/Rainfall..

....

Date Bloomed/Harvested ....

Notes ....

....

....

Rate It: (1)   (2)   (3)   (4)   (5)

❧ PLANT LOG ❧

PLANT NAME ....

SCIENTIFIC NAME ....

Flower ☐ Vegetable ☐ Fruit ☐ Herb ☐ Shrub ☐ Tree ☐

Annual ☐ Biennial ☐ Perennial ☐ Seedling ☐ Bulb ☐

SUPPLIER .... **COST** ....

Date Germinated .... Date Planted ....

Location .... Sun ☐ Partial Sun ☐ Shade ☐

Fertilizer/Soil Amendment ....

Pests/Weeds/Control ....

....

Watering/Rainfall..

....

Date Bloomed/Harvested ....

Notes ....

....

....

Rate It: ❨1❩ ❨2❩ ❨3❩ ❨4❩ ❨5❩

✽✽✽ PLANT LOG ✽✽✽

PLANT NAME ....

SCIENTIFIC NAME ....

Flower ☐ Vegetable ☐ Fruit ☐ Herb ☐ Shrub ☐ Tree ☐

Annual ☐ Biennial ☐ Perennial ☐ Seedling ☐ Bulb ☐

SUPPLIER .... **COST** ....

Date Germinated .... Date Planted ....

Location .... Sun ☐ Partial Sun ☐ Shade ☐

Fertilizer/Soil Amendment ....

Pests/Weeds/Control ....

....

Watering/Rainfall ....

....

Date Bloomed/Harvested ....

Notes ....

....

....

Rate It: (1) (2) (3) (4) (5)

PLANT LOG

PLANT NAME ....

SCIENTIFIC NAME ....

Flower ☐ Vegetable ☐ Fruit ☐ Herb ☐ Shrub ☐ Tree ☐

Annual ☐ Biennial ☐ Perennial ☐ Seedling ☐ Bulb ☐

SUPPLIER .... **COST** ....

Date Germinated .... Date Planted ....

Location .... Sun ☐ Partial Sun ☐ Shade ☐

Fertilizer/Soil Amendment ....

Pests/Weeds/Control ....

....

Watering/Rainfall ....

....

Date Bloomed/Harvested ....

Notes ....

....

....

Rate It: ① ② ③ ④ ⑤

⊰⊰⊰ PLANT LOG ⊱⊱⊱

PLANT NAME ....

SCIENTIFIC NAME ....

Flower ☐ Vegetable ☐ Fruit ☐ Herb ☐ Shrub ☐ Tree ☐

Annual ☐ Biennial ☐ Perennial ☐ Seedling ☐ Bulb ☐

SUPPLIER .... **COST** ....

Date Germinated .... Date Planted ....

Location .... Sun ☐ Partial Sun ☐ Shade ☐

Fertilizer/Soil Amendment ....

Pests/Weeds/Control ....

....

Watering/Rainfall ....

....

Date Bloomed/Harvested ....

Notes ....

....

....

Rate It: (1) (2) (3) (4) (5)

~ PLANT LOG ~

PLANT NAME ....

SCIENTIFIC NAME ....

Flower ☐ Vegetable ☐ Fruit ☐ Herb ☐ Shrub ☐ Tree ☐

Annual ☐ Biennial ☐ Perennial ☐ Seedling ☐ Bulb ☐

SUPPLIER .... **COST** ....

Date Germinated .... Date Planted ....

Location .... Sun ☐ Partial Sun ☐ Shade ☐

Fertilizer/Soil Amendment ....

Pests/Weeds/Control ....

....

Watering/Rainfall ....

....

Date Bloomed/Harvested ....

Notes ....

....

....

Rate It: 1 2 3 4 5

❦❦❦ PLANT LOG ❦❦❦

PLANT NAME ....

SCIENTIFIC NAME ....

Flower ☐ Vegetable ☐ Fruit ☐ Herb ☐ Shrub ☐ Tree ☐

Annual ☐ Biennial ☐ Perennial ☐ Seedling ☐ Bulb ☐

SUPPLIER .... **COST** ....

Date Germinated .... Date Planted ....

Location .... Sun ☐ Partial Sun ☐ Shade ☐

Fertilizer/Soil Amendment ....

Pests/Weeds/Control ....

....

Watering/Rainfall...

....

Date Bloomed/Harvested ....

Notes ....

....

....

Rate It: ❶ ❷ ❸ ❹ ❺

✦✦✦ PLANT LOG ✦✦✦

PLANT NAME ....

SCIENTIFIC NAME ....

Flower ☐ Vegetable ☐ Fruit ☐ Herb ☐ Shrub ☐ Tree ☐

Annual ☐ Biennial ☐ Perennial ☐ Seedling ☐ Bulb ☐

SUPPLIER .... **COST** ....

Date Germinated.......................... Date Planted ....

Location .... Sun ☐ Partial Sun ☐ Shade ☐

Fertilizer/Soil Amendment ....

Pests/Weeds/Control ....

....

Watering/Rainfall..

....

Date Bloomed/Harvested ....

Notes ....

....

....

Rate It: (1) (2) (3) (4) (5)

ꙮ PLANT LOG ꙮ

PLANT NAME ....

SCIENTIFIC NAME ....

  Flower ☐ Vegetable ☐ Fruit ☐ Herb ☐ Shrub ☐ Tree ☐

  Annual ☐ Biennial ☐ Perennial ☐ Seedling ☐ Bulb ☐

SUPPLIER .... **COST** ....

Date Germinated .... Date Planted ....

Location .... Sun ☐ Partial Sun ☐ Shade ☐

Fertilizer/Soil Amendment ....

Pests/Weeds/Control ....

....

Watering/Rainfall ....

....

Date Bloomed/Harvested ....

Notes ....

....

....

Rate It: (1) (2) (3) (4) (5)

~ PLANT LOG ~

PLANT NAME ....

SCIENTIFIC NAME ....

Flower ☐ Vegetable ☐ Fruit ☐ Herb ☐ Shrub ☐ Tree ☐

Annual ☐ Biennial ☐ Perennial ☐ Seedling ☐ Bulb ☐

SUPPLIER .... **COST** ....

Date Germinated.................................... Date Planted............................

Location .... Sun ☐ Partial Sun ☐ Shade ☐

Fertilizer/Soil Amendment ....

Pests/Weeds/Control ....

....

Watering/Rainfall..

....

Date Bloomed/Harvested ....

Notes ....

....

....

Rate It: (1) (2) (3) (4) (5)

✿✿✿ PLANT LOG ✿✿✿

PLANT NAME ....

SCIENTIFIC NAME ....

Flower ☐ Vegetable ☐ Fruit ☐ Herb ☐ Shrub ☐ Tree ☐

Annual ☐ Biennial ☐ Perennial ☐ Seedling ☐ Bulb ☐

SUPPLIER .... **COST** ....

Date Germinated .... Date Planted ....

Location .... Sun ☐ Partial Sun ☐ Shade ☐

Fertilizer/Soil Amendment ....

Pests/Weeds/Control ....

....

Watering/Rainfall...

....

Date Bloomed/Harvested ....

Notes ....

....

....

Rate It: (1) (2) (3) (4) (5)

🌿 PLANT LOG 🌿

PLANT NAME ....

SCIENTIFIC NAME ....

Flower ☐ Vegetable ☐ Fruit ☐ Herb ☐ Shrub ☐ Tree ☐

Annual ☐ Biennial ☐ Perennial ☐ Seedling ☐ Bulb ☐

SUPPLIER .... **COST** ....

Date Germinated .... Date Planted ....

Location .... Sun ☐ Partial Sun ☐ Shade ☐

Fertilizer/Soil Amendment ....

Pests/Weeds/Control ....

....

Watering/Rainfall ....

....

Date Bloomed/Harvested ....

Notes ....

....

....

Rate It: (1) (2) (3) (4) (5)

✿✿✿✿ PLANT LOG ✿✿✿✿

PLANT NAME ....

SCIENTIFIC NAME ....

Flower ☐ Vegetable ☐ Fruit ☐ Herb ☐ Shrub ☐ Tree ☐

Annual ☐ Biennial ☐ Perennial ☐ Seedling ☐ Bulb ☐

SUPPLIER .... **COST** ....

Date Germinated .... Date Planted ....

Location .... Sun ☐ Partial Sun ☐ Shade ☐

Fertilizer/Soil Amendment ....

Pests/Weeds/Control ....

....

Watering/Rainfall ....

....

Date Bloomed/Harvested ....

Notes ....

....

....

Rate It: (1) (2) (3) (4) (5)

PLANT LOG

PLANT NAME ....

SCIENTIFIC NAME ....

Flower ☐ Vegetable ☐ Fruit ☐ Herb ☐ Shrub ☐ Tree ☐

Annual ☐ Biennial ☐ Perennial ☐ Seedling ☐ Bulb ☐

SUPPLIER .... **COST** ....

Date Germinated .... Date Planted ....

Location .... Sun ☐ Partial Sun ☐ Shade ☐

Fertilizer/Soil Amendment ....

Pests/Weeds/Control ....

....

Watering/Rainfall ....

....

Date Bloomed/Harvested ....

Notes ....

....

....

Rate It: (1) (2) (3) (4) (5)

PLANT LOG

PLANT NAME ....

SCIENTIFIC NAME ....

Flower ☐ Vegetable ☐ Fruit ☐ Herb ☐ Shrub ☐ Tree ☐

Annual ☐ Biennial ☐ Perennial ☐ Seedling ☐ Bulb ☐

SUPPLIER .... **COST** ....

Date Germinated .... Date Planted ....

Location .... Sun ☐ Partial Sun ☐ Shade ☐

Fertilizer/Soil Amendment ....

Pests/Weeds/Control ....

....

Watering/Rainfall ....

....

Date Bloomed/Harvested ....

Notes ....

....

....

Rate It: (1) (2) (3) (4) (5)

✿✿✿✿ PLANT LOG ✿✿✿✿

PLANT NAME ....

SCIENTIFIC NAME ....

Flower ☐ Vegetable ☐ Fruit ☐ Herb ☐ Shrub ☐ Tree ☐

Annual ☐ Biennial ☐ Perennial ☐ Seedling ☐ Bulb ☐

SUPPLIER .... **COST** ....

Date Germinated .... Date Planted ....

Location .... Sun ☐ Partial Sun ☐ Shade ☐

Fertilizer/Soil Amendment ....

Pests/Weeds/Control ....

....

Watering/Rainfall ....

....

Date Bloomed/Harvested ....

Notes ....

....

....

Rate It: (1) (2) (3) (4) (5)

✿✿✿✿ PLANT LOG ✿✿✿✿

PLANT NAME ....

SCIENTIFIC NAME ....

Flower ☐ Vegetable ☐ Fruit ☐ Herb ☐ Shrub ☐ Tree ☐

Annual ☐ Biennial ☐ Perennial ☐ Seedling ☐ Bulb ☐

SUPPLIER .... **COST** ....

Date Germinated .... Date Planted ....

Location .... Sun ☐ Partial Sun ☐ Shade ☐

Fertilizer/Soil Amendment ....

Pests/Weeds/Control ....

....

Watering/Rainfall ....

....

Date Bloomed/Harvested ....

Notes ....

....

....

Rate It: (1) (2) (3) (4) (5)

~~~ PLANT LOG ~~~

PLANT NAME ....

SCIENTIFIC NAME ....
    Flower ☐ Vegetable ☐ Fruit ☐ Herb ☐ Shrub ☐ Tree ☐
    Annual ☐ Biennial ☐ Perennial ☐ Seedling ☐ Bulb ☐

SUPPLIER .... COST ....

Date Germinated .... Date Planted ....

Location .... Sun ☐ Partial Sun ☐ Shade ☐

Fertilizer/Soil Amendment ....

Pests/Weeds/Control ....

....

Watering/Rainfall ....

....

Date Bloomed/Harvested ....

Notes ....

....

....

Rate It: (1) (2) (3) (4) (5)

✤✤✤✤ PLANT LOG ✤✤✤✤

PLANT NAME ....

SCIENTIFIC NAME ....

Flower ☐ Vegetable ☐ Fruit ☐ Herb ☐ Shrub ☐ Tree ☐

Annual ☐ Biennial ☐ Perennial ☐ Seedling ☐ Bulb ☐

SUPPLIER .... **COST** ....

Date Germinated .... Date Planted ....

Location .... Sun ☐ Partial Sun ☐ Shade ☐

Fertilizer/Soil Amendment ....

Pests/Weeds/Control ....

....

Watering/Rainfall ....

....

Date Bloomed/Harvested ....

Notes ....

....

....

Rate It: (1) (2) (3) (4) (5)

ᔔᔔ PLANT LOG ᔔᔔ

PLANT NAME ....

SCIENTIFIC NAME ....

Flower ☐ Vegetable ☐ Fruit ☐ Herb ☐ Shrub ☐ Tree ☐

Annual ☐ Biennial ☐ Perennial ☐ Seedling ☐ Bulb ☐

SUPPLIER .... **COST** ....

Date Germinated.................................... Date Planted.....................................

Location .... Sun ☐ Partial Sun ☐ Shade ☐

Fertilizer/Soil Amendment ....

Pests/Weeds/Control ....

....

Watering/Rainfall..

....

Date Bloomed/Harvested ....

Notes ....

....

....

Rate It: (1) (2) (3) (4) (5)

❧❧ PLANT LOG ❧❧

PLANT NAME ....

SCIENTIFIC NAME ....

Flower ☐ Vegetable ☐ Fruit ☐ Herb ☐ Shrub ☐ Tree ☐

Annual ☐ Biennial ☐ Perennial ☐ Seedling ☐ Bulb ☐

SUPPLIER .... **COST** ....

Date Germinated .... Date Planted ....

Location .... Sun ☐ Partial Sun ☐ Shade ☐

Fertilizer/Soil Amendment ....

Pests/Weeds/Control ....

....

Watering/Rainfall...

....

Date Bloomed/Harvested ....

Notes ....

....

....

Rate It: (1) (2) (3) (4) (5)

~ PLANT LOG ~

PLANT NAME ....

SCIENTIFIC NAME ....

Flower ☐ Vegetable ☐ Fruit ☐ Herb ☐ Shrub ☐ Tree ☐

Annual ☐ Biennial ☐ Perennial ☐ Seedling ☐ Bulb ☐

SUPPLIER .... **COST** ....

Date Germinated .... Date Planted ....

Location .... Sun ☐ Partial Sun ☐ Shade ☐

Fertilizer/Soil Amendment ....

Pests/Weeds/Control ....

....

Watering/Rainfall ....

....

Date Bloomed/Harvested ....

Notes ....

....

....

Rate It: (1) (2) (3) (4) (5)

✿✿✿✿ PLANT LOG ✿✿✿✿

PLANT NAME ....

SCIENTIFIC NAME ....

     Flower ☐   Vegetable ☐   Fruit ☐   Herb ☐   Shrub ☐   Tree ☐

     Annual ☐   Biennial ☐   Perennial ☐   Seedling ☐   Bulb ☐

SUPPLIER .... **COST** ....

Date Germinated .... Date Planted ....

Location .... Sun ☐   Partial Sun ☐   Shade ☐

Fertilizer/Soil Amendment ....

Pests/Weeds/Control ....

....

Watering/Rainfall ....

....

Date Bloomed/Harvested ....

Notes ....

....

....

Rate It: (1)   (2)   (3)   (4)   (5)

PLANT LOG

PLANT NAME ....

SCIENTIFIC NAME ....

Flower ☐ Vegetable ☐ Fruit ☐ Herb ☐ Shrub ☐ Tree ☐

Annual ☐ Biennial ☐ Perennial ☐ Seedling ☐ Bulb ☐

SUPPLIER .... **COST** ....

Date Germinated .... Date Planted ....

Location .... Sun ☐ Partial Sun ☐ Shade ☐

Fertilizer/Soil Amendment ....

Pests/Weeds/Control ....

....

Watering/Rainfall ....

....

Date Bloomed/Harvested ....

Notes ....

....

....

Rate It: (1) (2) (3) (4) (5)

~~~~ PLANT LOG ~~~~

PLANT NAME ....

SCIENTIFIC NAME ....

Flower ☐ Vegetable ☐ Fruit ☐ Herb ☐ Shrub ☐ Tree ☐

Annual ☐ Biennial ☐ Perennial ☐ Seedling ☐ Bulb ☐

SUPPLIER .... **COST** ....

Date Germinated .... Date Planted ....

Location .... Sun ☐ Partial Sun ☐ Shade ☐

Fertilizer/Soil Amendment ....

Pests/Weeds/Control ....

....

Watering/Rainfall ....

....

Date Bloomed/Harvested ....

Notes ....

....

....

Rate It: (1) (2) (3) (4) (5)

✤✤✤ PLANT LOG ✤✤✤

PLANT NAME ....

SCIENTIFIC NAME ....

Flower ☐ Vegetable ☐ Fruit ☐ Herb ☐ Shrub ☐ Tree ☐

Annual ☐ Biennial ☐ Perennial ☐ Seedling ☐ Bulb ☐

SUPPLIER .... **COST** ....

Date Germinated.. Date Planted ....

Location .... Sun ☐ Partial Sun ☐ Shade ☐

Fertilizer/Soil Amendment ....

Pests/Weeds/Control ....

....

Watering/Rainfall..

....

Date Bloomed/Harvested ....

Notes ....

....

....

Rate It: (1) (2) (3) (4) (5)

✿✿✿✿ PLANT LOG ✿✿✿✿

PLANT NAME ....

SCIENTIFIC NAME ....

Flower ☐ Vegetable ☐ Fruit ☐ Herb ☐ Shrub ☐ Tree ☐

Annual ☐ Biennial ☐ Perennial ☐ Seedling ☐ Bulb ☐

SUPPLIER .... **COST** ....

Date Germinated .... Date Planted ....

Location .... Sun ☐ Partial Sun ☐ Shade ☐

Fertilizer/Soil Amendment ....

Pests/Weeds/Control ....

....

Watering/Rainfall ....

....

Date Bloomed/Harvested ....

Notes ....

....

....

Rate It: (1) (2) (3) (4) (5)

～～～ PLANT LOG ～～～

PLANT NAME ....

SCIENTIFIC NAME ....

Flower ☐ Vegetable ☐ Fruit ☐ Herb ☐ Shrub ☐ Tree ☐

Annual ☐ Biennial ☐ Perennial ☐ Seedling ☐ Bulb ☐

SUPPLIER .... **COST** ....

Date Germinated .... Date Planted ....

Location .... Sun ☐ Partial Sun ☐ Shade ☐

Fertilizer/Soil Amendment ....

Pests/Weeds/Control ....

....

Watering/Rainfall ....

....

Date Bloomed/Harvested ....

Notes ....

....

....

Rate It: (1) (2) (3) (4) (5)

﹏﹏﹏ PLANT LOG ﹏﹏﹏

PLANT NAME ....

SCIENTIFIC NAME ....

Flower ☐ Vegetable ☐ Fruit ☐ Herb ☐ Shrub ☐ Tree ☐

Annual ☐ Biennial ☐ Perennial ☐ Seedling ☐ Bulb ☐

SUPPLIER .... **COST** ....

Date Germinated .... Date Planted ....

Location .... Sun ☐ Partial Sun ☐ Shade ☐

Fertilizer/Soil Amendment ....

Pests/Weeds/Control ....

....

Watering/Rainfall ....

....

Date Bloomed/Harvested ....

Notes ....

....

....

Rate It: (1)   (2)   (3)   (4)   (5)

❧❧❧ PLANT LOG ❧❧❧

PLANT NAME ....

SCIENTIFIC NAME ....

Flower ☐ Vegetable ☐ Fruit ☐ Herb ☐ Shrub ☐ Tree ☐

Annual ☐ Biennial ☐ Perennial ☐ Seedling ☐ Bulb ☐

SUPPLIER .... **COST** ....

Date Germinated .... Date Planted ....

Location .... Sun ☐ Partial Sun ☐ Shade ☐

Fertilizer/Soil Amendment ....

Pests/Weeds/Control ....

....

Watering/Rainfall ....

....

Date Bloomed/Harvested ....

Notes ....

....

....

Rate It: (1)   (2)   (3)   (4)   (5)

PLANT LOG

PLANT NAME ....

SCIENTIFIC NAME ....

Flower ☐ Vegetable ☐ Fruit ☐ Herb ☐ Shrub ☐ Tree ☐

Annual ☐ Biennial ☐ Perennial ☐ Seedling ☐ Bulb ☐

SUPPLIER .... **COST** ....

Date Germinated .... Date Planted ....

Location .... Sun ☐ Partial Sun ☐ Shade ☐

Fertilizer/Soil Amendment ....

Pests/Weeds/Control ....

....

Watering/Rainfall..

....

Date Bloomed/Harvested ....

Notes ....

....

....

Rate It: (1) (2) (3) (4) (5)

ꙮꙮꙮ PLANT LOG ꙮꙮꙮ

PLANT NAME ....

SCIENTIFIC NAME ....

Flower ☐ Vegetable ☐ Fruit ☐ Herb ☐ Shrub ☐ Tree ☐

Annual ☐ Biennial ☐ Perennial ☐ Seedling ☐ Bulb ☐

SUPPLIER .... **COST** ....

Date Germinated... Date Planted.............................

Location .... Sun ☐ Partial Sun ☐ Shade ☐

Fertilizer/Soil Amendment ....

Pests/Weeds/Control ....

....

Watering/Rainfall..

....

Date Bloomed/Harvested ....

Notes ....

....

....

Rate It: (1) (2) (3) (4) (5)

GARDEN PLANNING
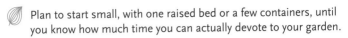 SUGGESTIONS AND TIPS

- Plan to start small, with one raised bed or a few containers, until you know how much time you can actually devote to your garden.

- What kind of garden interests you? Flowers, ornamental plants, herbs, vegetables, fruits? A water garden? A rock garden? What about a butterfly or pollinator garden?

- Do you want to attract wildlife? Or are you concerned about deer, rabbits, and other creatures consuming your plantings?

- Where will you put your garden? If it's easily accessible and in a place where you can see it every day, you will be inclined to spend more time there.

- Consider how much sun your garden space receives. Many plants need six or more hours of sun per day.

- Do you have a source of water close by? Or will you have to irrigate via a hose or a watering can?

- Garden smart. Keep in mind your hardiness zone. Find out average frost dates. "Go native" and choose plants that will thrive in your area, in your specific gardening space. You'll save on water and fertilizer, cut down on weeding, and have fewer pests.

- Plan. How high will your plants grow? You don't want tall plants to shade shorter ones.

- Will you be able to access your entire garden to water, weed, and fertilize? Make a path if you can't reach plantings in the middle.

- Are you planting herbs and salad greens you'll harvest often for meals? Plant them within easy reach.

- Do you need to budget for plants, tools, and supplies? Where will you keep your tools and supplies?

- Get your soil tested to learn what nutrients it contains (or lacks) and to find out its pH levels. pH levels are measured from zero (most acidic, or "sour") through 14 (most alkaline, or "sweet"). Most plants prefer a neutral pH level of about 7. Soil testing kits are available at home and garden centers. Lime improves overly acidic soils. Sulphur improves overly alkaline soils. If you decide to make use of soil amendments, follow package directions.

- You can also amend garden soil with compost. Start composting with a compost bin or tumbler, available at home and garden centers. Add "brown" material, like leaves, straw, and wood chips, and "green"material, like salad and veggie trimmings and coffee grounds. (You'll be impressed with how much less trash you generate.) Moisten dry materials. Stir or tumble the compost regularly.

- Use plastic-free starting materials, or start plants in clean, dry eggshells (the shells will contribute calcium to the soil). Poke holes in the bottom for drainage.

- Or use bathroom tissue tubes to help get plants started. Cut slits around one end of each tube and fold inward to create a bottom. Add soil and plant seeds. When it's time to transplant, set the entire tube in your planting bed; the cardboard will disintegrate.

- Water planters without losing dirt out of the bottom by laying a coffee filter inside.

- When you water, do so in the morning, as less water will evaporate.

- Consider using a barrel or trash can to collect rainwater from your home's downspouts for garden irrigation. Search online for implementation ideas.

- Have container plants? Check containers often in hot weather, as soil can dry up quickly. Hanging baskets may need water daily.

- Take houseplants outside in late spring for a summer vacation. Keep them in partial shade to avoid sunburn. Bring them back inside in September. Check for insects first and re-pot as needed. Note: Shorter days and decreased light will now slow their growth; they'll need less water and fertilizer.

- Let tomatoes ripen on the vine as long as possible. Refrigeration disrupts the process and affects flavor negatively.

- Donate surplus fruits and veggies to local hunger and homeless outreach programs.

- Before winter, drain your hose. Clean and oil tools.

- Rinse empty flowerpots. Soak in a 10 percent bleach solution. Rinse again and dry. Wash your garden gloves.

- Planning to purchase a live Christmas tree and plant it after the holidays? Dig the planting hole beforehand and fill with straw and mulch until it's time.

- Avoid using salts that melt ice and snow near lawns, plantings, and garden beds, or use vegetation- and pet-friendly ice melters.

- Take a gardening class in winter. Request seed catalogs or shop online. Plan next year's garden. Start a new garden logbook!

MONTHLY GARDENING TIPS

- The United States: The **Old Farmer's Almanac**, www.almanac.com/gardening/tips and **Better Homes & Gardens** magazine, www.bhg.com/gardening/gardening-by-region/

- The United Kingdom: The **Royal Horticultural Society**, www.rhs.org.uk/advice/in-month/

- Australia: **Sustainable Gardening**, www.sgaonline.org.au/monthly-guides/

HARDINESS ZONE INFORMATION

Will your plant withstand your winter? Find out with the **United States Department of Agriculture Plant Hardiness Zone Map** (see next page), the standard by which you can determine which plants are most likely to thrive. The map, last updated in 2012, is based on the average annual minimum winter temperature, divided into 10° Fahrenheit zones. If you visit the USDA website here: planthardiness.ars.usda.gov/PHZMWeb/, you will be able to enter your zip code to find your exact hardiness zone.

The **American Horticultural Society** also offers a **Heat Zone Map** to help you determine if your plant can withstand summer's hottest temperatures. You'll find it here: www.ahsgardening.org/gardening-resources/gardening-maps/heat-zone-map

Canadian gardeners: Visit the **Department of Canada Agriculture and Agri-Food** website for an interactive plant hardiness map: sis.agr.gc.ca/cansis/nsdb/climate/hardiness/index.html

Those in the **United Kingdom** may visit the **Royal Horticultural Society's** website for a chart of hardiness ratings here: www.rhs.org.uk/plants/pdfs/rhs-hardiness-rating.pdf

Australian gardeners may visit **Australian National Botanic Gardens'** website for a hardiness map: www.anbg.gov.au/gardens/research/hort.research/zones.html

International gardeners may also visit the following sites for additional hardiness zone maps and gardening information:

 www.plantmaps.com

 www.backyardgardener.com/garden-forum-education/hardiness-zones/plant-hardiness-zone-map/

 www.gardenia.net/guides/climate-zones

U.S.D.A. HARDINESS ZONES

Average Annual Extreme Minimum Temperature 1976 to 2005

ZONE	TEMPERATURE (DEGREES FAHRENHEIT)
1a	-60 to -55
1b	-55 to -50
2a	-50 to -45
2b	-45 to -40
3a	-40 to -35
3b	-35 to -30
4a	-30 to -25
4b	-25 to -20
5a	-20 to -15
5b	-15 to -10
6a	-10 to -5
6b	-5 to 0
7a	0 to 5
7b	5 to 10
8a	10 to 15
8b	15 to 20
9a	20 to 25
9b	25 to 30
10a	30 to 35
10b	35 to 40
11a	40 to 45
11b	45 to 50
12a	50 to 55
12b	55 to 60
13a	60 to 65
13b	65 to 70

GENERAL HARDINESS ZONES OF SELECTED U.S. CITIES

Note: Most cities have multiple zip codes. Enter your exact zip code on the U.S.D.A. website (https://planthardiness.ars.usda.gov/PHZMWeb/) for precise hardiness zone information.

City	Zone	City	Zone
Amarillo, Texas	7a	Little Rock, Arkansas	8a
Anchorage, Alaska	4b	Los Angeles, California	10b
Annapolis, Maryland	7b	Louisville, Kentucky	6b
Atlanta, Georgia	8a	Miami, Florida	10b
Billings, Montana	4b	Missoula, Montana	5b
Birmingham, Alabama	8a	Mobile, Alabama	8b
Bismarck, North Dakota	4a	Montpelier, Vermont	4b
Boise, Idaho	7a	Nashville, Tennessee	7a
Boston, Massachusetts	7a	New Orleans, Louisiana	9b
Buffalo, New York	6a	New York, New York	7b
Caribou, Maine	4a	Oklahoma City, Oklahoma	7a
Casper, Wyoming	5a	Pensacola, Florida	9a
Cedar Rapids, Iowa	5a	Philadelphia, Pennsylvania	7a
Charleston, West Virginia	6b	Phoenix, Arizona	9b
Chicago, Illinois	6a	Pierre, South Dakota	4b
Columbia, South Carolina	8a	Plattsburgh, New York	5a
Columbus, Ohio	6a	Portland, Oregon	8b
Concord, New Hampshire	5b	Providence, Rhode Island	6b
Dallas, Texas	8a	Raleigh, North Carolina	7b
Denver, Colorado	5b	Reno, Nevada	7a
Dover, Delaware	7a	Richmond, Virginia	7b
Duluth, Minnesota	4b	Sacramento, California	9b
Flagstaff, Arizona	6a	Salt Lake City, Utah	7a
Green Bay, Wisconsin	5a	San Francisco, California	10b
Harrisburg, Pennsylvania	6b	San Juan, Puerto Rico	13a
Hartford, Connecticut	6b	Santa Fe, New Mexico	6b
Honolulu, Hawaii	12b	Savannah, Georgia	8b
Indianapolis, Indiana	6a	Seattle, Washington	8b
Jackson, Mississippi	8a	Shreveport, Louisiana	8b
Kansas City, Kansas	6a	Spokane, Washington	6b
Laredo, Texas	9a	Springfield, Illinois	6a
Las Vegas, Nevada	9a	Topeka, Kansas	6a
Lenox, Massachusetts	5b	Trenton, New Jersey	7a
Lincoln, Nebraska	5b	Washington, D.C.	7a

GARDEN PLANNING
GRID PAGES